"Yes, but . . ."

Also by Arthur J. Stewart

Rough Ascension and Other Poems of Science

Bushido: The Virtues of Rei and Makoto

Circle, Turtle, Ashes

The Ghost in the Word

From Where We Came

Elements of Chance

The Hallelujah Series and Other Poems

Uncoils a Snake

Logjam

"Yes, but . . ."

Poems by Arthur J. Stewart

Periploi Press
NASHVILLE, TENNESSEE
2024

Copyright © 2024
First edition

All rights reserved. No part of this publication may be reproduced, stored in a retrieval system, or transmitted in any form or by any means—electrical, photocopy, recording, or others—except for brief quotations in written reviews, without the prior written permission of the publisher.

Cover art, titled "Left Brain, Right Brain,"
was created by artist Bonnie M. Lewis
Design and editing by Dariel Mayer

Manufactured in the United States of America

The author did not knowingly use artificial intelligence (AI) tools in creating this book.

ISBN: 979-8-9857833-6-0

Library of Congress Control Number: 2024919920

"What's it all mean, Bill?
What's it all mean?"

From W.J. Matthews and E. Marsh-Mathews. 2017. *Stream Fish Community Dynamics: A Critical Synthesis*, chapter 9. Johns Hopkins University Press, Baltimore, MD. 330 p.

"Where to Go," was originally published in *The Hoosier Science Teacher*, 47(1), 2024 .

Contents

Preface ix

Write Like You Mean It 1
We All Walked 2
Tap-tap-tap 4
Enough Is Enough 6
Prognosticators of the Weather 7
So Many Questions 8
Do It Anyway 9
Like Jackstraws 10
So Awkward 11
Mary Oliver, in "Deep Summer,"
   on Observing a Mockingbird 12
Six Voices 14
Details 17
Working from a Writing Prompt 18
Yes, but… 21
Beyond "Yes, but" 48
On Becoming 49
As You Go 50
Core 51
Change 52
Donating 53
The Ornamental Plum Tree 54

Where Are You?	56
Structured	57
Absolving	58
Looking for the Good Stuff	59
Learning to Sink	60
Transitions	61
Where to Go	62
The Future	63
This Happened	64
The Artist Father Framing	66
Life as a Frothy Tug	67
Big Hope	71
About the Author	72

Preface

When trudging the slow, long-haul path of becoming a poet, a writer inevitably finds themselves asking:

> where do poems come from: you may
> want to know: have you ever wondered
> …
> wonder which comes first, the motion
> of feeling, or the event, the perception,
> connection: oceanward, you could
> say that a rift of motion starts in
>
> the doldrums, forms a progression… [1]

All developing poets need to inspect this question, as did poet Archie Ammons, who put his voice to the matter in *Glare*. The question needs to be addressed in pieces because poems come in a multitude of ways—in short, intense bursts, like gamma rays from a neutron star, or more gently, like the slow uncoiling of memories and longings; they come in lines, words, pastiches, or quilt-squares; like water over rocks, or dew on grass, or like an unhurried in-depth inspection of a rose's green-thorned stem. It's all different. It's always different. But if a poet considers the way a poem or group of poems emerges, she or he sometimes can begin to tap the creative source: they then can prompt it, encourage it, and stand back, giving the inkling room to grow. That poking, inspecting, and studying—that is the process I used in creating this book.

    I have long enjoyed Ammons' rollicking language, the sudden dips and sways, his careful but devil-may-care attitude, the way he bounced his thoughts from stanza to stanza, in constant motion. In fact, several years ago I paid tribute to his poetic skills in a chapbook, *Uncoils a Snake* [2], but here, I'm in a different mode. Yes, I still greatly appreciate and admire his work, but I'm trying to get through it; get over it; and move on. I am trying to grasp the essence of the world from my vantage and our places in it through more independent eyes.

    I developed the long central poem in this collection, titled "Yes, but…"

using Archie Ammons' book *Glare* to provide a sequence of writing prompts. The core of "Yes, but…" centers on negotiation—a thing we do constantly, a thing we must do, minute by minute as a way to fit into the world. It is about how we reconcile one thought with another, with attention given to how things fit. It is about how one person responds to another person's point of view, as they both continue to adhere to their own point of view and their own set of facts. "Yes, that is true, but…"

We do it second by second, all the time, with others and with ourselves. At least, I think this is true, but…

To satisfy my innate fondness for both chaos and order, in this longish poem I started with *Glare*, page 3. There, I skimmed words and phrases that caught my fancy—"boulder from the blue," "wandering stone," things like that. And then I wrote from my heart, lines that were triggered by the prompting words. Next, to address my insatiable need for ordered disorder, I skip-hopped forward, selected a new page, and again wrote to prompting words and ideas found there. By repeating this process multiple times, I ended up working through the entire text of *Glare*, pausing sometimes to contemplate and create, in an effort to capture my overall sense of *Glare*.

Now, that's it. I think I'm done with Archie. Peace be with you, good Buddy.

But then briefly back again, to more accurately explain this collection: in addition to the poem "Yes, but…," this collection includes a series of short poems that frame my little window to the world. Through these shorter works, my intent was to begin breaking down the structuring aspects of science that have organized my life, and to begin devoting myself instead to a more science-free view of the world. My aim here is to explore things bounded more by a simple holistic sense of beauty and emotional completeness, and infused with a little humor. The world, after all, is a funny place. So I offer several shorter poems leading to the core poem, "Yes, but…" — and then follow "Yes, but…" with another series of shorter poems, which open onto my new post-Ammons path. In this preface, you can see that I've inverted concepts, as often I do, to create a personally satisfying end to my singular attraction to Ammons' works, and then to set out on a new journey.

1. Ammons, A.R.1998. *Glare*. W.W. Norton & Company, New York, NY. 294 p.
2. Stewart, A.J. 2021. *Uncoils a Snake*. Periploi Press. Nashville, TN. 46 p.

"Yes, but . . ."

Write Like You Mean It

1.
I try not to stuff
poems with parenthetical material,
or half-words, or too many things
set off in italics. If you want
to say something, just say it—
to hell with niceties. Most platitudes went out
in the seventy's for good reason. There's just
too much to do.

2.
And don't get me started
on repetition—it's good
sometimes if used rarely, but rarely good.

3.
A smattering of stuff
on the page for spatial emphasis—that can work.
   In-
dents, extra blank lines,
very short lines

mixed erratically with long lines, sometimes OK
but less good.

4.
Work the verbs.
Enjamb
everything
(football, stiff arm), use

funky punctuation
or sometimes none, cheesy tricks
of the trade.

We All Walked

a long time and
the five of me grew
gradually tired
together. Some of us

sat for a while: one began whittling
a little wood whistle from a willow whip
and he made it make

high-pitched squeals like a
pink curl-tailed
piglet at the county fair.

Another one went on,
a long way, now and again
squealing wee wee wee—,
small, just like
      the goat-
footed balloon man,
far

and the last three
finally agreed: we no longer knew
what to do, what
to do. Puzzling
did not resolve things:
the contemplations
were too deep,
the paths were too narrow

    and, besides,
just look:
water in the bountiful creek
continues curling down
under the steady force
of gravity, mass striking mass,
moment wrapping empty moment.
Night comes at last and the sky
grows dark slowly
and stars
began falling,
falling, resting
on the water's surface

Tap-tap-tap

Mid-morning, writing. Tap-tap.
Tap-tap-tap-tap.
Something, some
little living thing, rustling
now and again and tapping,
a distraction

at my upstairs office corner,
thirty feet above the ground,
near where electric lines
arch across the sky
from the road, and enter the house

around the corner: but I could not see

even after opening
        (*tap-tap-tap tap*)
the window to better
peer out. But I had to know:

if squirrel, he or she would soon become
a pellet-gun goner—nope,
sorry, but I can't allow
squirrels nesting in the attic, chewing

white and black insulated wires
to bare copper. So I hasten

downstairs, slip
through the front door, turn left,
quiet-step
to the corner,
under the holly-tree, thick prickle-
leaves, peer up

up up to discern
at last slight motion. Ah,
a Downey. That's OK mostly.
Tolerable at least. So I dislodged

his bug-eating
efforts with a hurled pine cone.
That action made tap-tap go

but you see, disruption won.

Enough Is Enough

There's not enough time left
to do much of anything except to breathe

love into the world, with each
remaining breath. Calculating,

I may have 3 million breaths left,
perhaps a few more

or a few less, before the heart
stops and the little prayers end.
But who counts

that way? Perhaps
we should count
like the little pond-turtle counts, the one now poking
his olive-green and yellow-striped head

up from the water's surface, looking
for his favorite half-submersed log;

or the slippery frog, motionless
in the sun on his favorite lily pad—

or not count at all.

Prognosticators of the Weather

They huddled briefly, big-eyed and nervous, looking
for confirmation and harmony.
But they hesitated and grew confused.
Wetlands dried and forests shrank to grasses;
Oceans waves kept slipping

over sand on beaches, and the water continued
curling under bare toes. But it was warm.

Too warm, even for conchs,
oysters and lobsters. The deserts began blooming
with heat: the wavering air
packed up and moved south
in a huff. Birds
became dizzy; they hung
upside down by their feet from branches and barked

like tree frogs. The frogs
tried hard to grow wings, but they failed.
White chickens
strutted past a red
wheelbarrow glazed with rain, admiring
their individual profiles in the adhered drops;
they clucked as they passed, as if
it was important.

But now back
to the prognosticators
huddled in confusion:

one
somehow grew bold and began
asking questions.
She saved the world.

So Many Questions

If you just ask
(who) for help
(doing what?)
will it (help)
happen or not?

But it's not
that simple: it could be
you'll just get
more comfortable
with asking for more

rather than wanting less.

Do It Anyway

Each day I move
from problem to problem
to problem; there's no

easing off, there's no
getting things done, and some days
I am so tired I could weep. Now

I'm putting hardware cloth
around the base of our new shed
to hopefully

exclude skunks and ground-
hogs; the U-shaped staples
get hammered in tight;

the cut wires poke the hands; the back
and neck muscles knot
hard to pain, odd angles, crouched low

I discover
few problems ever get solved;
they just morph

so they look new.

Like Jackstraws

I don't want to dream
an old man's dream.
But now, that might be
all I can do. Gone,

the spritely flowers, the soft
green twigs of spring; gone,
summer's heat—great
cumulonimbus clouds rising

in late afternoon, flattening as they touch
the stratosphere: distant
mutter of thunder, the first
hint of cooling breeze. And now,

autumn: leaves
beginning to turn, and they will turn
colors hard after the first frost. They will turn

as I turn now, glancing
over my right shoulder. The years
pile like jackstraws: none

can be pulled individually from the heap, none
can be inspected
in isolation. They are lodged

firmly, each one
resting upon another,
        dreaming
about when they were new,
so neatly bundled.

So Awkward

Death is so awkward.
Yet we keep doing it—
at least once per person.
It's awkward

for the person dying
and anyone nearby, because
we're not quite sure

what it means
or what to do about it.

Cry, sometimes. Feel sad,

often. Happy, less often.
But awkward, always.

If we're very close to it
we may gently close the eyes
that now can't see

or say or think a small prayer.
But please withhold
loud wailing or grieving.
After all, even though awkward,

death is an opportunity
to forgive; it is a chance
to help the living

set things straight.

Mary Oliver, in "Deep Summer," on Observing a Mockingbird

"Your clocks, he says plainly,
which are always ticking,
do not have to be listened to.
The spirit of his every word."

And that's true.
We have twenty-two clocks, if you count
digital time-keeping devices such as computers
and cell phones. And nine of these
are ticking and they keep ticking

due to tension: springs and gravity.
Plumb-weights for the cuckoo clock,
and also for the grandfather clock,
and the mantel and regulator clocks.
The weights drive the pendulums
by gravity and they exert control

through shining gears
and cunning mechanisms.

So I find myself
listening to them.
One, for example, is about a minute slow
when striking the hour; another
is a minute or two too fast.

I spend time
correcting them: halting, for a moment,
those that are running fast, and
advancing the minute hand

slightly for those that are running slow.
On the hour
the house is a cacophony of
bongs, chimes, bells,

and cuckoos.
But the mockingbird would say, correctly,
I listen to the wrong things.
He would say my life is a mess.

Six Voices

1.

Yes, Mary Oliver,
that's exactly the way to put it—

like a hinge opening
and closing, sealing
one part of my life
behind me, another part
opening to sudden light
like a day-lily opens,

certain, clear, and compelling.

But I fear I will not be here
long enough to see that.
Not long enough, in any case,
to reliably count
the number of crepe myrtle flowers
on just one sturdy limb.
Not long enough to see
next fall the first few flocks of Canada geese
winging south in large Vs, the leaders
steady in their resolve,
pushing forward,
forward with measured wing-beats,
one strong stroke after another.

2.

Charles Bukowski asked,
"I wondered when and where
I might finally come to rest and then
fit in."

The fitting in—that's the hard part.
Who is it that melds
the many rough- and sharp-edged
fragments of life that can't fit
without heat, to make
just one magnificent thing
from the many?

3.

William Carlos Williams said
of leafless vines in winter,
"They enter the new world naked,
cold, uncertain of all
save that they enter."

And that's true. But how do they depart?
Not with a rush,
not with a bang,
not even with a whimper.
Perhaps it is only the world that leaves them,
their small bodies, dry stems.

Hush now, nibbling fears.
Day by day the barren vines
are getting clipped; have faith,
I said: there will be fruit aplenty.

4.

Something as precise
as a name sounds right: something
clear as a noun or a well-chosen verb.

Theodore Roethke, lost
as the last son, said
"Snail, snail, glister me forward,
Bird, soft-sigh me home,
Worm, be with me.
This is my hard time." And it was,

and still is—even for thousands more
with lesser voices. But Rumi,
bless him, said it best:
"Every word / I say opens into mystery. Any /
way I turn I see brilliance."
And that thought should prevail.

Details

Line breaks are such
funny things—they
can make

or break a poem, de-
pendng on where

you put 'em.

Working from a Writing Prompt

Such long words, such long lines and long
sentences: it's tough to escape
that type of poem—one just gets
dragged in, willy-nilly, and you must
participate: join the party, wave,
or clap and chant, nudge
someone standing near you, encourage them

indirectly to mountains of relief when the
convention's finally over, when
the shopping's done; when,
after the long hike, you have
opportunity to sit and rest the feet.

This poem will be a wild one, I hope: one
that wanders, sometimes leading and
sometimes trailing
far behind: a stump-like
welter of words, condoned or not, fluffy

and soft or solid: one can't work
or walk in a stream here,
the motion's not right, the pace is wrong,
not even a few slippery rocks

for water to burble around, or stroke
thin fins of the small trout, gills
methodically moving, pulsing
life, as it hunkers, almost
motionless despite

water pressing along the lateral lines. They are
so delicate: the trout's thin-scaled body

responds to the gentlest change
of pressure with change in depth. So

should I

let it take me that way? Move left? Prepare
to dive deeper, get ready to feel
the slight pressure-push
of encouragement, letting me know,
        it's OK to forget
           the above: it's OK to forget

the sensuous push of sunlight,
the smallest breeze that swirls
surface debris—fragments of dead leaves, a scuff
of flotsam, pollen in spring, traces
of an organic waste that in fact
is not waste, not
in the least: it will be
re-used
like star-dust, *ad infinitum*.

And if I wanted to write
    just
     one
      more

poem, what would be the topic? Or
the point? After all
has been said
and mostly done, many poems

are not read at all; most books

do not become famous; most books
deserve what they get
in the great scheme of things and

we don't matter much either—
in most cases, we matter
much less than we think we should,

but a few do. Like presidents
are remembered by name, even if
they're scoundrels at heart: they also go
the way I'll go, if they're lucky, down
the slippery slide of old age gathering

speed, dust and cobwebs, a head-knock
or two, without fanfare or glitter of glory
which I don't really want.
It's OK to finish last:
there's no medal for the winner.

Yes, but...

(*Glare* page 3)

Wouldn't it be grand, grand
beyond speculation
if destiny's stone just missed us: if it
skimmed by, silent and spinning slow and
just
kept
going. We,

in joyful puzzlement might then
look back and see
being silly can be serious:
furrow the brow, puff
out the rosy cheeks, see

Glare for what it is: so small, but oh,
such a grand construction, snapping up
bits and pieces, arguments pro and con and I say
damn, Archie, you did a grand thing.
Being silly

is half the way to knowing—it
        stretches
ways of knowing. We could
get with the program, find those

lapses and leaps, discover
new ways to think and more ways
to be silly. Tools can help. My favorite
is an eight-foot length of #9

steel rebar:
heavy, simple, but good

for so many things: a lever-arm—a pry-bar,
or smashing deck-wood boards to bits

I've used it to pry up
a big ole zero-turn Toro mower, lever it
onto blocks to get
to the blades; and to pry up
pre-cast concrete steps for leveling,
things like that: it's easy peasy to
pop off deck boards

during a deconstruction project:
jam it twixt adjacent boards, rest
the fulcrum point on a joist,
push down and

up she comes. So, Archimedes:
your observations, set to practice.

Yes, but

it's easy to wander accidently:
let's get back to *Glare*. Archie claimed
falsely his life of service drained him, yet

there he went, one, one, old or no, still
going, still pushing, being snotty
sometimes, elegant others, mostly
truthful, making messes, obviously

screwed up too, but
just
kept
going,
putting ink to paper and salt
and pepper to egg. What if

(*Glare* page 23)

instead I just hopped around, pausing
here and there in *Glare*, to pick up
odd-bob bits and pieces, random pages
like little nits, but always going forward, aiming
for a lumpy time-line, a pastiche:

an itchy scalp, a day
in second grade, or when you thumb
your nose at other poets, bold shame
on you. Constraints
consistently generate
such curious effects, hit or miss. Thinking

back, speculation is close to speculated
close to speckle, dotted
eyes and cross your t's. Brings up
a memory, hunting whiptails: beautiful

creatures, like their name, slender and
with pointed snouts, slinking

under bushes and around rocks, day-
warming in the Sonoran Desert, west and south
of Phoenix, far up, blotted blur from haze,

but down, the whiptail, sliding shadow
under greasewood, palo verde, creosote
bush: try to noose one with waxed string tied
near the tip of a car's radio antenna—again
and again, sneak a step, good luck: like truth,

it's almost always
six inches out of reach. Archie
seemed to have favored brooks and streams,
talked less
about creatures living there
although sometimes he did

(*Glare* page 32)

Approximating
is a useful skill, and with that plus a few
memorized numbers you're
good to go. Twenty drops of water
is about a milliliter; a nickel

weighs about 5 grams. A gallon of water
weighs about 8.34 pounds, there's
28.3 grams per ounce, it takes
2.47 acres to make a hectare.
It's like going

from Sanskrit to German
or from Portuguese to French, wouldn't you
like to be able to do that
now and then, just for fun? Navigate, getting

from one place to another,
that can be a task—a tisket,
a tasket and so forth: and so sorry, I don't know
the etymology of that. Maybe

he did, or maybe I should
approximate history, or look it up,
or make it up. Some do. After all,
it's the little things that count.

And that talus of incidentals:
       or talons,
like those of an osprey,
digging deep into the white flesh

of a foolish fish, swimming too near
the surface of a lake, silly thing,
thinking, maybe, a bug was there to eat
dimpling the surface, a small out-flooding

series of rings, or something
like that, some small cool
fishy thought. But it's gone now: it became

    (*Glare* page 47)

An odd predilection
for meteor-linked catastrophes;
or for example, when the Earth
blobbed up, lost the moon. But why boots

crusted with evil?
I'm not so sure about that
or the purported benefits of couplets, time
and again, although they help

intensify fragmentation. Even if
fragments are all in truth we have

and good luck with that thought too.
I'll go back to four or more for now: too much

dichotomy spoils the soup, sours
the stew: see, S's are so easy, they sway.

Early in *Glare* he worms
his way toward *Garbage*,

it's easy to tell. He said, set out by
the street in clever plastic lid-lockable
big containers, and a big truck—
not much
doubt about that, but look, he wrote this

in 1997 or earlier, whereas
Garbage came out in 1993, what the heck:
    it's all
backwards again. Yes, but that's normal:

he was a slippery crawdad
and pinchy too.

    (*Glare* page 65)

food for nestlings in a sticky nest: not sticky
as in related to coefficient of friction,
or resistance to slide, or intensity of
adhesion but rather, sticks—

beak-picked bits of wood.

So now, here it is, late
November, almost December, ice
should be on the pond, or hard starry frost

on windows, or icicles, or sleet, but no,
not a bit of that: we're struggling
with seventy degrees, leaves
on various trees finally gave up and came down

anyway, so there's still things to do. But it's all wrong.
We've whoppered the big circle;
there's no going back, it's just a hard pull
from now on. Think about the farmers.

    (*Glare* page 77)

he declared
he had a long history of misery.
Well, we all do
what we can with what we have

and his misery (if that's what it was)
profligated (if that's the right term)
some damned good books. Wish
I could do that with my misery—
don't you?

(*Glare* page 83)

napping is right next door
to snapping, one can do
one or the other, probably not
both at the same time. Things

get so dichotomous: turn
left here, turn right here, despite
spooky action at a distance, but
we've got a whole 360 degrees

or more I guess of choice, is that
dichotomous too? Maybe it devolves
to half-degrees, or tenths
or maybe an infinitude of more.

I don't do good snapping, better napping.

(*Glare* page 93)

Some metaphors are pure
spectacular: try the one in which
he notes he can't go down the road straight:
a wheel comes off and flies
across a pond, the hood
flaps away to Mars, the seats disjoint, soon
he's riding a chassis like a Greek chariot,

plunging
downhill to a bifurcation. Well,
that's what it's all about:
that's what happens
when you write

poetry, the
bifurcations: and the plunges,
of course. Each time

I feel lucky to be alive.

    (*Glare* page 95)

The chrysanthemums in the pot
out front were
bright yellow, pure
bee-bait two weeks ago;

but they got too dry, lost their luster,
they're going now
hard to seed, maybe the roots
still have a little gnarly life, and there

it is again: the wander-job, the sleazy slip
from where we were away to where
we want to go, the navigational problem.
The moon tonight is pure half-faced

sallow, unkempt, not
like the beauty of a full moon
or a new moon, one that lets
stars glitter in the background dark

and not
the skinniest moon
you can imagine

just looking, it could be going
either way, how
can one know for sure?

or six or seven
lines per stanza, whatever
number works out right
to carry on the thought or
give one studied pause.

(*Glare* page 100)

Filler, much more than needed
to span the gap between
where one idea trails off
and another gets picked up,

a roadside carcass. I see
many here, especially if one
roadside or the other is lined with trees;
tree-type doesn't matter much:

squirrels, skunks of course, the occasional
opossum, now and then
a coyote, a buck or a doe
all odd-angles, often hit
multiple times, a flattened

furry mess hell why can't people learn
to drive, or do they
aim sadistically on purpose? Not wise
to aim for skunks. And going too fast,
not nice, skunks in particular
make bad filler

Yet all goes down, all goes
round and round, whoppered
or not. Buzzards fatten, raise
their gnarly heads
take one step back
when the next car comes.

(*Glare* page 106)

Special commentary: I've read
the book so many times the pages

are starting to fall out, getting

unglued I guess: more note-
worthy than a gentle flower-wander,
or an off-target take on quiet birds.

    (*Glare* page 117)

A few good lines like
"woggle: the birch bunch tips over
to the ground: the shrubbery skews"—
things like that

pepper the palate and make it all
good
better
best

    (*Glare* pages 127-130)

body bent to the cane is a good one too
but then it's back to filler ,
we're peeling
meaning off, layer by layer,

onion-like, compare that to a peach,
dare I? Not. I don't need
another weather report, that changes
every day although through time

it all blurs, fogs over, gets static:
decomposes
to numbers on a chart and
true: obfuscation
is not good cover for mystery: I mean
what should we do

    for example
about UFOs or UAPs: some of those
films are damned impressive

and and and mysterious
and some are not
clear, or are clearly fakes. That's

nothing but perverse
think about it
and add 'or adoration'

    (*Glare* page 136)

It's good to let a little
natural stuff help hold

the hill together: else, con-
sider the larger-scale con-
sequences: organic things

misplaced can rot
ferment, fluster buster clear down
to methane, that stuff's 24 times
worse than CO_2, what should one

do with that? In some
cases the solution
to pollution might be dilution
when you truly can't

do a better thing: Fukushima for example

bad from the get-go
assumptions approximations proclamations
    all balled up
together with obfuscations
let that rot: leaves, OK:
a slow spin down, shield
the grass, bye and bye
they, too, will go

still a worry: should that be by?

    (*Glare* page 145)

A look-back: it looks like too many
right-hand looks: odd numbered
noted pages predominate, maybe
I should practice looking left.

But considerable consideration
caught my eyes (both)
right or left, right
or wrong. Correctly put,

you'd be surprised
how little something can be and be
better than nothing:
even a thing as thin

as a thin soup to a hungry man

Slurp
And a little dribble

    (*Glare* pages 151-159)

And yes, the drowsy
disengagement of incompletions:
well, I'm right there, buddy,
weather reports or no

not much to win
means not much to lose
if things
at the roots are circular

but incompletions dominate,
so much effort goes

to avoidance, maybe better
bite the bullet, give up

hope for the possibility of glory:
and yes that delicious dark
permeating, penetrating, some
places so dark even stars can't

shine through: now that's a bad line

too predictable. So it goes
next to crows
fluttering high and casually as if
they don't care where the hell they are

or are going: he just snaps over
idea to vision to concept
to actual thing in one hop;
that route risks stranding a lot of

unused fuel
and when it's gone
bud it's gone,
no getting it back

to know you is
to appreciate
what you tried to do
while knowing

nothing is immortal
but water is
not alive but dances, sprays: rock
resistance and gravity,

sun-driven at the core
as are we all, you said it best
we glisten, glisten

(*Glare* pages 174-176)

crack of innocence, cluttered
despair, a thing forgotten
won't come back: so move along
bud: leave a gap, move on

sometimes just find the right
word to hold space and it starts working
again: the thing
gets hard, erect

a plausible argument or forget:
then come
up with a suitable alternative or
get out of Dodge before

sunset: owls and all, after all:
and words are just words,
don't hang your shingle out too soon
sometimes cooling is

the gracious thing to do.
Gracious
how you made that weird jump
at the end. Funny

how a small percentage
of a big number is a big number.
Taxes for example. Not the same
as texts—dissimilar

(*Glare* pages 182-183)

About light and water: the way
light plays on water, but mostly if
a tiny breeze makes ripples then
the angles change as if

by magic: angelic, no? He festers
a flock of nuanced words, some
fret for freedom but they're roped down
solid; square knots not bowlines.

So right or wrong, what's
the difference, is it
enough to worry about. Science
after all is said and done is

a guessing game with numbers.

(*Glare* pages 185-187)

Use a natural image of nature to
ramp things up, get'er going
fast enough to spin off towards
where you want to go presuming

there is a want and that idea begs the matter
where does want
come from? I mean
hunger, sex, temperature

(too hot or too cold) water
of course, legitimate wants coalesce to needs
but there's that other
kind of thing: a vaguer thing,

an urge, a slow burn
like over-used
pectoral muscles after an hour
of hoeing. Or raking.

That low desire: that's the type that
drags one out, makes one want to
dust off the dust,
jeans or no, boots or shoes, probably

even barefoot, the toes
crinkling on new grass, oh
joyful, makes me think of spring.
And gardening. Years ago

I roto-tilled up the biggish
garden plot in spring, great soil, planted
two long rows of corn, feeling
lucky (against raccoons later; they'll

crawl up and husk the forming ears,
nibble kernels
off the cob, go on to the next
over and over) and

eight days later the little spears
were coming up, up, bold,
thinking hard and snitching sun,
and a bastard flock of seven crows

marched the two rows in morning,
tugging one after another
the spears up to get
to the rooting seed, the emerging

bit of green life going up, root down
and guzzling it. I shot at them
from a second-story window, a
long-rifle 0.22—my old

Stevens model 87D, bang
but missed. Yet OK, despite
the 70-plus percentage loss;
those shining black-feathered varmints

smart enough to not come back.
The tomatoes, zukes, and cukes survived.

And that's enough. Squeaky wheels
or weeky squeals are good to share.

    (*Glare* pages 193-195)

Such a glorious outpouring
of fine words: mouthfuls, chewier than grits
age stacked up behind, fewer
years ahead before the big

event we all await
outside the edge of normalcy;
hoping
for a surprise and then being
surprised when it happens.
Expectations can be so
outrageous, so lofty a large

bird could not get that high—run out
of steam, physiologically speaking, oxygen,
invisible stuff like
hope, gobbled up day after day and

where does that get you: better
to tone it down, take a deep
breath. Yes
but all in all we still want.

There's not a spec of I here
and that's OK: one can still
plan a future, frame it, even if it doesn't
work out.

    (*Glare* pages 200-202)

Whirling the drain, going
faster as the circles close: a fine

image, and likely it sports
a certain truth, a notable

thing, secular or not, that's
purely a judgment call and such call
is itself secular by nature. But I believe
in a certain religiosity, not so much

in schooling: that's a place for facts it's a place
for one to think about that: which place
deserves one kind of thinking, which place
is the place you want to live and try

mightily to keep the two places
separate: don't mix mustard and chocolate
gasoline and fire, vinegar and ice cream
or sherbet, Neapolitan or other: the lime

is best in my opinion and I've heard
like a mouth, everyone has one
or more of those. If we didn't we'd be
in a pickle. So much of what is

is unknown, beans
black, kidney, even cannellini or no
and I like the cannellini
best in chicken soup.

With a touch of lemon.

    (*Glare* pages 212-213)

Funny how he dug down,
gave up, went to weather
I've done that thing before as well
mostly in letters, it gives

a body time to think and boy
that's a little thing we all should do
more of; perhaps this is
an example of bad writing, just slipping

a letter or two out of place and talking
like mad about the purported
consequences of said change, bantering
about until finally at last

getting to the core of the thing: the damned
universe again, it doesn't matter if you look at it

with the Hubble
or the James Watt Space Telescope
regardless of wavelength, infrared to hard
violet, almost violent it's so chock full
of energy the place
after all is just the place and we are
so small within it—smaller
than bits of dust
into which we will go down
to hell
with flesh-flabby dugs, he said things
like that to smooth out

the larger complexities. Even the future
little tasks seem little, brittle, pre-fabricated,
made up.

       (*Glare* pages 220-221)

Wow.
What a run-down, a serious
explanation of what happens
during decrepitude and when I

used that word, too, explaining
self conditions to my doctor he
just laffed, said things weren't yet
quite as bad as that. I wonder if they teach

those things in med school. Later
at least he (not the doctor) brings us back
to age ten a time when
we all have such a narrow view of saved

at about that age my dad
in a '56 Chevy with bald tires and
a predilection for making oily smoke
stopped by a tent revival: I had no idea

what was going on, just
followed him in and stood
in back at his side and heard
and saw a multitude of fluttering

things: loud shouting call-outs, Jesus
this and that, come on up
and be saved, stuff like that with

people in fold-up wooden chairs bobbing
and weaving, crying out
I thought like a nighthawk
Giving those sudden beeps at dusk, flying

almost bat-like against the night-dimmed
sky. He said

nothing to me about that
ever after; just wanted me to see
and hear a thing like that, suck it in
figure out

what to do with it and
years later I'm still
not
quite
sure

    (*Glare* pages 223-224)

Wiggles into the thing
again round-about, half-clothed,
half-assed before he really
really gets going. So what

I'm familiar with trying
to understand conversations stuffed
with ambiguous pronouns
fancy that,

bulging and all,
battle or not

    (*Glare* pages 231-233)

The beginning of a beginning
wanders on stage, un-
remarkable, not beginning
with a great idea, a wondrous
what-if or do-you-suppose

a science-bludgeoned question
generally of little value in the long
run, from some far-upstream river bend
to here, breeze-directed flotsam
slipping along the shore

yeppo: keep closed

the writers' room door, keep close
its little specificities, the most
minute details of

scissors pencils pen all shoved
crammed point(s)-down in a hand-
thrown pottery cup
two rolls of old Scotch tape in
separate dispensers, one
heavy as sin, the other too light to work well
and papers piled

just so and half a dozen open books

and

letters I should have responded to
         but have not yet
had the time
although I suppose

I would have had I thought
it was especially important to do so.
Some
might rightly say you lazy bastard, get
more things done, quit
just screwing around, putting up
dishes, doing the laundry whatever

from now on

every second is precious, every
moment is momentous, every
itsy bitsy fleck of time
when it's gone it's gone

at least for me. After all, who knows

what really happens

(*Glare* pages 238-239)

Bedazzled by his own words but going
he claimed to light and airiness,
emptiness, less grain, rolled
oats perhaps rather than wheat
or chaff, and burrows

on rocky paths.

BULL SHIT

(*Glare* pages 240-241)

Well, right there anyway—right
about being or not being
a scientist. That sure caught
my eye, caused me to dangle
in part on that word evidence because

that's all we do look listen
sniff the air like a hound, con-
sider the facts, con-
template the possibilities using that little

causal analyzer thing in the head, the thing
that, spinning, generates
a small hypothesis about what's what, what's
coming next, or if uncertainty still prevails,

go, fetch more data We do that
instant by instant, evaluating
the world in its multitude
of voices. Buddy

it's the sun, fusion-mobbed blob
of hydrogen, helium and heat
what makes things meander round and
round, you said so

earlier. don't
go back on your words now, or
stick them into useless crannies.

HELLS BELLS

    (*Glare* pages 249-250)

Almost a point, could be a flinty
stone-bit or rough-cut shard
of obsidian, slick as a head
fresh shaved bald. Go a

head, snatch out the space, make a thing of it
that it's called knapping, clever word look
suitable for a warthog wallow in a bit
of dust or muddy detail, it all works out

forget a thing and after a while it will
(usually)
come back, rearing up on its little
pair of hind legs begging attention.

NITROUS OXIDE MIGHT HELP

    (*Glare* page 261)

The fork problem
in spades applied
ever which way; the slow sink
to oblivion, the story

(if there is-was one) long gone
moldy, molted, immolated
at last setting free the carbonaceous matter
as a gas. We know

how to do those things, understand
(mostly)
how a few things got
to where they are, even the bells

and whistles, by a hard narrow stare at genes
how proteins fold, dynamics
of ectoplasmic manifestations
(not) electrons scuttering

(a crass blend
of scattering and scuttling)
by detailed modeling and
heaven forbid, AI.

Fictitious
sometimes interesting
always

      (*Glare* pages 272-273)

Nearing the end now, almost
time to take a breath, pull
back, ask hard what's
the question, put a question mark

on that if you please. Like marmalade
on buttered French bread toast. Well,
we're well into Part 2 Scat Scan just in case
you've been tracking place and keeping pace

and still I'm hard a'looking for the
big message, the Great Prompt
the ever-elusive

whatever it is that drives us
out of the forests, into the plains

into and out of caves, huts, sod-
covered outposts, rough

log cabins, tidy little Cape Cods
curled up here and there, like
at Martha's Vineyard and other
places routinely pounded by Nor'easter
storms, wind, rain. Yes, but

not finding it
here or there: nothing formulable
enough to be taught
is worth teaching—straight his words,

except for the rare
possibility of grace in redrawing the line.

    (*Glare* page 281)

Giving up
a conclusion,
don't
ask me

(*Glare* pages 293-294)

So this is it—the
last chance, the dice-roll, the
end of the line, the

nebulous upholdings,
snake-eyes,
        the cock
waggling a breeze on the weather-vane
looking vainly for north,
high up on the barn-roof,
just above a bay
door to the loft, hay
bales visible stacked neatly, one

after another
Yes, but
who would have thought

grass could be that tough: or wheat straw,
or (laf-laf) alfalfa

MUCH MORE NUTRITIOUS

Beyond "Yes, but"

> Over and over I wonder:
> is what I've done so far
> good enough to justify
> my life?
> My efforts
>
> seem so small,
> the world is so big.

On Becoming

Each day
I am becoming smaller
and thinner, verging now
on transparency. Each day
I know less and less,
and soon—
too soon, it seems—
I will become

just a pin-prick
in the universe. No,
something
much smaller than that.

As You Go

If you get tired, or lonely,
know this: yes, the trek is long

but rewarding. On the way
you'll meet many others,

some of which become
dear friends. When you become

too hot or too tired to continue,
take a break; it will not hurt

to pause and review
life and your accumulating story.

Core

Stepping back
from the edge of the core
I stand confused,
with the wild wind whipping
my thinning hair.
I am perplexed

about everything—things
known and things
unknown;
things bleak or holy. For example

grass does not grow much
in winter, and it can look dead
but it's not. Its roots

cling to soil, saving its life.
Like something in me
clings to hope, here
at the maelstrom's edge.
Can I cling

to the belief
things will get better?

Change

You want change?
This
is how it happens.
      Beauty
leads to hope;
      hope
leads to faith;
faith
leads to confidence,
and confidence
leads to action.
  So just look
for beauty in the world.

Donating

It starts
with a long list
of questions: over the past
six months have you ever
over the past
three months have you done
any of these things, or have you been
here or there?

When at last the needle slides in
it doesn't hurt much. Blood flows
down the tube
into the plastic bag. Just
fifteen minutes, maybe twenty. Perhaps
it will save someone's life.
Perhaps it won't.
Do it
because it might.

The Ornamental Plum Tree

Today, to be kind, I stopped
at a neighbor's house
just up the hill and knocked
until she came
to the door yawning and rubbing

sleep from her eyes and I asked

would you like me
to cut down and saw up
your ornamental plum tree, that one
right there, in front, by the road? It's been dead

for nearly a year and
I have a good chain saw—
I could do it
in just a few minutes

for free. You know, being
a neighbor and all.

But she demurred, noting
that that tree had been her tree, with
special branches, years before and

it didn't seem right yet
to cut it. But she would (and she did)

call her mom to ask advice
and when she came back to the door

where I stood, patiently looking
at the dead tree, noting

a dozen easy cuts and it would be
ready to stack, rough short logs,
right there by the side of the road

but she reported
the mom said no,
not yet.

Where Are You?

We're here
for such a short time.
Why not
be thoughtful,
loving,
kind?

Structured

Before me,
a path, well-trampled:
weeds crushed
to earth, and bare earth
in some spots to mud.

Clearly it has been used
by others on their way
through life to death.

I dare not
look too hard to the left
or to the right—there's so many
interesting things to do
with the time remaining

whatever amount is left.

Absolving

Oh, what a wonderful
word! Now
if we can just
do it

fairly, without
malice, without
sequestered blame, without
expectation
of return, we'd

be so much better off.

Looking for the Good Stuff

If you chose to not dig,
you can chose to sink

or hold perfectly still
and let things burble up

on their own accord.
Try it. A cup of tea might help,

or a brief nap, or something
taking almost no energy
from you—the rising
is the energy. Let it

push up, slowly, magna-like,
glowing in the dark

molten rock
deep in a volcano's throat.

Learning to Sink

Allow yourself
to sink

slowly, so as to feel
smooth bubbles
against your cheeks

and hear them
in their hasty rush up.

And as you settle
you may become sleepy.

But don't fall asleep.
Rather, pay close attention:
make sure

your eyes are wide open
and your heart, too.

you'll see
wondrous things
each day.

Transitions

Of all the years, this year
has been by far the fluffiest;
like pink cotton candy,
light as a cloud; the one

without clear shape or form; the one
like low fog in early morning,
when spring
decided to slyly slide in

around a corner and summer rose
like a soft rose; then autumn,
redundant, quiet as a leaf,
yellowed and fell.

Winter now
seeks uncertain toe-hold: its scratchy edges
scrabble at dawn's pink rim with
small hooked claws.

Where to Go

A small dark lump on the asphalt driveway this
morning as
the sun was working
over the eastern ridge, and the lump

moved a little, letting me know
it was alive. Stooping
close, I discovered the lump
was a fresh cicada,

and carefully picking it up, I found
the body was still
soft in places, but with
hardened transparent wings

and red eyes. It thrashed briefly
in my open hand as it tried at first to fly.
The pallid soft belly
glistened as the creature

righted itself, hesitated
and suddenly thereafter
buzzed off, up into the maple tree.
Unlike me it knew

exactly where to go.

The Future

Appears
and disappears
just
like
that: almost
a blur, with time

a massive locomotive
roaring along, cinders flying
and stubby plumes of
wind-swept smoke and steam
pressing,
pressing to get out, the great
wheels
churning, the wheels
driven hard by the massive push
and pull of

the pistons, the piston rods and
the main
and eccentric rods, all
connected cleverly with purpose,
motion
influenced by the lead
engineer: he above, silent, attentive,

attuned to each unusual
hiss of stream or creak or groan of
metal strain. Destiny

from one
vanishing point to another,
planned and hoped.

This Happened

While we were standing
at a street corner, waiting

to cross
a rough-looking

black man with coarse
features was there too:

but not waiting

to cross: just waiting
in his wheel chair, with all

his personal belongings tied
onto it in plastic bags, and he

now and again burst
into loud talk, speaking to

someone we couldn't see
and his gnarly hands

moved almost on their own
as he talked, ignoring

us, and he got busy
ripping off a large clear plastic bag

he had jerry-rigged into a
primitive parka; got busy tearing off

most of the thing finally but

a blue and white scarf, held
at first in his lap

slithered down as he worked
his arms, and it

fell
partway to the ground and as he

maneuvered the chair
back and forth a bit

as we waited and as
he waited, the scarf

tangled in the smaller wheels,
obstructing progress, but he

paid no attention to that
as he broke

again into loud talk,
gesturing

and I wondered where was
a sister, a brother, some-

one, anyone
to help him with his

schizophrenia

but exactly then a cloud broke
open and sunlight

streamed down his craggy
face, and the red light

changed to green.

The Artist Father Framing

He worked hard
to make a 45-degree angle
with no protractor: the frame
must be his, just as the picture was. Until,
as last resort, he solved
the problem: folded
paper, dotting ends of the framing wood
with a coarse pencil
sharpened with a used
single-edged razor blade.
      But then
the miter box was cheap
and the saw it held could not
track the line as finely as needed
for good framing. So
Elmer's glue mixed with sawdust
mostly filled the gaps. And then, the matt:
strips of burlap, cut and
glued to Masonite.
      The result
was not nice, but functional:
he declared victory.

Life as a Frothy Tug

1.

surging now and again to crest
the waves, the hull
wave-battered yet still strong and
the diesel roar sometimes muted as the
prop goes deep
enough to catch hard the water,

there being not as rough, more
stabilizing, and holding
tight
(but not too tight, not tight enough
to slow the
inevitable). Tug
nosing closer, edging, bumps and roars
pushing hard the big thing oh, such a small
amount. Once—

it seems a hundred years I
calm now at the thought then of
doing something great; thought
as a youth spurred by
the empty threat of praise you'll do

something great, we have
no idea but so much
confidence in not knowing
what that thing will be: over

and over despite
my asking again and again
not that: lost
in a sea, an ocean

of complexity, surface waters racing
this way and that, pitched
high, then low, then high

on each ascending descending
crest or trough, pitching, until finally

only utter loneliness was big enough
to cover all the facts
soaked up while
looking
looking.

2.

So babbles the moon
from its pox-marked face
curling each month
to a sneer
or a grin; gradually

even this thought moves
from I through something
to you: else
it's no good: not

with agency, not mean-
ingful, no backbone,
       no
authentic spice. The words
rot on the vine. And con-
sidering spice, there's a vast

variety, allspice through za'atar, some
medicinal (see: crab-like, it works its way
one tight claw after another up
the slippery pier-post, but still
part of the ocean, the sea).

3.

When sliding on the continuum;
fog out the slender spikey times, the

abrupt sudden shocking

transformations of conditions—
memory
is not fast enough to
capture what did what,
what sprang, leaped or darted
across the path, was it

dark, hairy scaly smooth-
skinned or with feathers
things do that

constantly; most are
too small to see
but still
can be important. It's all

going somewhere at some
self-inflicted subtle pace
curling sometimes, or

almost straight sometimes
or as an arc. Abrupt
is its best descriptor, sense
of sudden alarm—attention, what

was that, what was

and back
to the great uncertain
in me, well yes with hard work later perhaps
I can prune this bitch life
to something
meaningful, but not yet.

Big Hope

When the time comes
and I start to drift,
I hope I'll see and say
"Oooh,
so *THAT's* how things work!
How beautiful!"

About the Author

Arthur Stewart's poems have been published in more than a dozen national and regional poetry anthologies and in various literary and scientific magazines, including *Rattle, Journal of the American Medical Association, Lullwater Review, Big Muddy, New Millennium Writings, Bulletin of the Ecological Society of America*, and *Chemical & Engineering News*. He was a 1997 Tennessee Poetry Prize winner, a 2009 winner of the Wilma Dykeman Prize for essay writing, and a 2013 inductee into the East Tennessee Writers' Hall of Fame for poetry. He was a writer-in-residence at Michigan State University's Kellogg Biological Station, and has given workshops on effective science writing for undergraduate, graduate and postgraduate science interns at U.S. Department of Energy facilities in Tennessee, West Virginia, Pennsylvania, South Carolina, Oregon and Colorado. *"Yes, but..."* is his tenth published collection of science-inspired poems.

For more information about this book or Arthur Stewart's other works, please contact the poet or his publisher at: *stewart.arthur.j@gmail.* or *periploi.press@gmail.com*

As the years pile up like jackstraws and lodge together, Stewart delves into his lifelong admiration for A. R. Ammons. With fresh, robust language and using *Glare* as a writing prompt, he shows us how "being silly can be serious," how "approximating is a useful skill," and how "bantering about until finally at last getting to the core of the thing" can become a joyful celebration of language and life. *"Yes but..."* is as playful and exuberant as it is wise.
  —Amanda Holmes, Read Me a Poem at *The American Scholar*

In *"Yes, but..."* Art Stewart reevaluates his relationship with several other poets, maybe taking a step back from reverence, and a step toward friendly criticism. After all, as the eponymous title of the central poem in the collection implies, there is often more to say on any subject. In the final set of poems, Stewart does say more—mostly about life and death, and love and kindness, and other mysteries. These poems are beautiful, and melancholy, but they leave the reader with the impression that the author remains hopeful (even optimistic) that a life spent in careful observation will ultimately be rewarded with understanding.
  —Mac A. Callaham, Jr., Research Ecologist, USDA Forest Service

Stewart, a scientist, bids farewell to Archie Ammon's unique poetry style by using selected slices from *Glare* as prompts for his own long poem, "Yes, but..." Then, hinting at future direction, Stewart includes a series of new non-scientific short poems which provide valuable insights into life. The book, *"Yes, but ..."* is an excellent resource for teachers and students exploring the various forms of poetry that have evolved throughout history.
  —Jim Johnston, author of *Exile Revisited*

In the book *"Yes, but...",* Arthur Stewart gives insight into how poets become inspired, sometimes by words and sometimes by thought. He creates poems from questions not answered from Archie Ammon's book *Glare*; he transcends *Glare* with his sharp wit and humor, and in so doing elevates his own poetry to a new level.
  —Walker Nowell, MD, Knoxville, TN

Made in the USA
Columbia, SC
10 October 2024

43434631R00055